INSIDE OUT UPSIDE DOWN ME!

MELISSA COETZER

© Melissa Coetzer 2021

Inside Out Upside Down Me!

Published by Melissa Coetzer

Durban, South Africa

Ultramel15@icloud.com

ISBN 978-0-620-92321-7

2 4 6 8 10 9 7 5 3 1

Cover graphic by Melissa Coetzer; model is Mia Coetzer

Layout by Boutique Books

Printed in South Africa

Welcome to the rambling forest of my mind,
where thoughts wander, and get lost!

CONTENTS

INSIDE OUT UPSIDE DOWN ME!

No more boxes

No more boxes
No more boxes for me
I can have foxes and rabbits,
Hats and habits – good ones –
But no more boxes for me

No more boxes! No more boxes!!
No more boxes for me.
I simply cannot be boxed
It's far too constrictive
Far too defining
The lines and the rules
Don't give me freedom to move
I want wings on which to soar
A voice that can roar
A head to stand tall
A box is just too small

No my dear, it's very clear
No more boxes for me

TEARS

They will not fall down my cheeks any more.
They are halted somewhere distant, in a far off place
Where the hunters go and do not always return.
They are buried in the forbidden land,
The one I shall not visit for I am but a girl.
Will someone collect them for me, I pray?
Bring them carefully back;
Put them in a bucket and do not spill a drop.
I will owe you a great debt
If this for me you will do.

HUNGRY

I am hungry for something,
I do not know what.
Feed me,
Do it straight from the pot:
But I don't want to lose my mind,
Lose control
Fade away,
Without my soul.
Where it goes, so must I!
Oh, darling, don't you cry.
I am not like you,
I know
I cannot follow you into the snow.
It might be white, it might be bright
But it's not the right kind of light!

I am afraid that my foot,
Though I lightly tread,
Will lead me to dread,
The day I go
And so…
I won't!

SHADOWS

Shadows of our former self, reflected in the mirror.
Shadows on the ground, on which I stand – give me your hand?
Shadows behind me, into whose darkness I fall.
Right there, up against the wall:
Shadows, looming tall,
Shadows making me small
I see shadows of a former self.
I look in the mirror and I see,
Me!

You may lose
everything

You may win a war
But lose a fight.
You may win tonight
But lose what's right.
Don't despair,
Just beware
What is hidden from sight.
Run now.
Take flight.

IMPRISONED

The bars to which I cling
Have become the very things that keep me in
Confined within my mind
A virtual prison

Who placed the bars and when?
And how did I come to see them as my friend?
Do they protect me from the big scary world in which I live?
Or do they just keep me from living?
Looking out while others look in, but don't really see
They feel pity, but not compassion, for the monkey in the cage

The monkey has become enraged
She is lashing out against the bars that confine her
But she does not know how to live without
    them and so she wants to run:
To run and leave it all behind!
It is just too hard, she thinks,
So she seeks refuge in the comforting words of strangers
Reaching out to them, only to discover that, although she
    thought she meant much, she means nothing at all

Where does that leave her?
What will she do now?
Oh monkey, you are not who you think you are

Saying goodbye I
Hold back a tear it will be
All right in the end

PAIN

There is so much pain
And nowhere to put it all
It's a burden that cuts to the core
Pain needs an outlet
Sport or Art
It needs to be hurled at something with passion
And left there with the sweat or the tears
Or the resultant masterpiece, the new creation

She is afraid of
the dark but she closes her
eyes when he kisses

THE PHOENIX

The phoenix rises from the ashes
What was broken, trodden on and crushed into dust
What was left lying on the ground,
Walked away from because it was no more
Has risen again!
From the ashes, a re-birth.
From the midst of despair
A fiery light leaps into the air.
The phoenix has risen,
Ablaze with new light,
Proud and fiery, to all a delight

THE PHOENIX

Broken, crumpled, left to dust
And yet still the fire smoulders
A burning inside that just won't die
And so she rises from the ashes
A blazing light, a phoenix
In full flight

CREATE!

Create
Draw
Write
Be
Inspired
Meander
Through
The portholes of your mind
Wash the pain away
With the comfort of your words

Let the dandelion whisper on the winds of
    your breath as you wish upon the air you
    breathe to sustain the life that you live.
Let your world be fragile, wobble a little like
    jelly; it is not always concrete, it is not always
    certain and it doesn't have to be.
Be someone's hero, be your own hero, be the kind of
    light you want to see in those around you.
Find joy in the small things, find joy in the small
    Joy you created, find your own joy.
When you are empty, open your eyes again to the sights,
    your ears to the sounds, be still and listen, listen
    for the beating of your own heart, the rhythmic
    sound – can you feel it? Can you even hear it?

Can you be that still?

Like a Mosaic
Broken pieces artfully
Arranged are me!

CONSISTENCE!

There is nothing consistent about me
I am as erratic as the wind
As wispy as the tendrils on a dandelion
My temperament
Patterned like the clouds
Light and airy
Or thickly covering the sun
Or non-existent
Just a pale blue sky
But where do I go
When I pull away
Retreat or hide
Lock myself in my mind
And is it safe?
For my mind is a minefield
Landmines planted strategically forcing me along old networks
Paths rooted and rutted with time and overuse
Worn bicycle tracks
Like those on the banks of a dry riverbed
Well-travelled
So, I must create new paths
Beautifully and artfully lined
With what draws in the breath
Closes the eye
Opens the chest
Expands the mind

Unexplored pathways
I must find my own happy place
My own ocean
That flows full and free

FEATHER

Softly you tickle me,
Feather
Gently you caress me,
Feather
Slowly you unravel me,
Soon you will tether me –
A bridle, a bit – and I
Will bite down so hard
As I scream
Inside
What begins so tenderly
Is just the start of the
Lie!

CAGED

My heart is caged in my ribs for its own protection.
If it were not it would flutter out,
like a bird with a broken wing,
it would stutter that it loves you
and what would that bring!

WINGS

My Wings
Unfold
Smack, the air cracks
Shake
Rotate shoulder blades,
Feel the movement
Push Back
Chest out
Head up
Head back
Arms open
Wide
Hands facing heaven
Eyes closed
Involuntary pulsing
Body restless
Wings flapping
Soar

LAST NIGHT

Last night I lay in bed in
Early evening darkness
The curtain, slightly open,
Reveals the garden beyond
A soft breeze blows gently
And fills the curtain,
Like a sleeping child's tummy,
Softly breathing in.
The tree outside is silhouetted against
The nearly fading light
A tranquil scene of pure delight

THE END

In the end there is only the end.
All the beginnings cease;
there are no more startings over.
No more second tries,
no more getting it right.
It's over, finished,
and all you can hope for is to be ready.
To have done enough forgiving,
enough uncomplicating,
enough living simply,
humbly,
patiently.
That you have been enough,
that it's been enough.
The end will come, of this we are certain.
Waste your time wisely then!

The sea surface, glass
Beneath a turbulent state
Mirrors emotions

RESISTANCE

A writer sits on grassy lawn as the sound of the ocean roars,
the gentle buzzing,
far off humming,
of a light aircraft in the distance.
The spray gently kissing her crossed legs,
not enough even to wet the pages of her book,
a fine sprinkling.
Two walls of sheer separated rock reveal the
        vista of the ocean before her.
 The sky a paler shade of blue,
is how it distinguishes itself
From the ocean,
a darker deeper blue.
Darker perhaps because of the secrets it holds,
in the depth of its belly.
The waves crash white,
angry.
A turmoil of emotions sits visible on the surface,
while below,
calm.
A rage that swirls and crashes,
rolls and starts again.
A constant thrashing,
as if it is fighting against itself,
against the rock,
against the space it's in.

It's being forced to stop,
when what it wants to do is continue,
but there is a wall of rock.
A barrier that won't allow it to,
and so, there is a rage against the finality of its end.

LET SLEEPING DRAGONS LIE

I live in a house on a hill,
but the hill is not really a hill
made of earth, sand or stone.
The hill is a dragon,
the scales on its tail the staircase to my house.
For years I have lived atop this sleeping dragon.
It's a beast, sure, and life is unstable, for when
    he stirs my foundations are shaken.
The glasses fall and shatter to pieces;
some things are repairable, others are not.
He cannot move without it having an
    impact on me in some way.
I should relocate, I know,
there are other places on which to build my home,
ones with solid ground.
It is not like I even get to appreciate the view on top of the hill,
I am too obsessed with the dragon below,
who sleeps contentedly!
HE is not affected at all by the structure on his back;
he is not even aware of my presence as I come
    and go about my daily business.
I do not exist in his contented world.
His sleepy existence is my wakefulness,
my punishment.

What will happen if he wakes?
I will be crushed and exist no more!
It is best to pack up and move now,
find a new place;
for my heart is my home.

SILENCE

Silence speaks its own language
Broken things belong
In the shadow of a mountain
One might feel small
But the looking up makes one tall
Stand and be
Take to the trees and see
Nature has a way of speaking to thee

What am I to do?
When I'm lying upside down
My smile turns to frown

A WRITER

I write therefore I am a writer
Self-doubt
Lucid thought
Pen in hand
Fluid movement
As it arches and weaves across
The page
With a life of its own
It must out
This story come
Here I am
Hear me now
Leave me not
Before I have
Captured you on paper
White and free
Then you are mine
For all eternity

EARTH, FIRE, AIR, WATER

Where are you now?
Where are you?
Will you still disturb my balance when I see you again?
Will earth lose its gravitational pull?
Will your fire consume or cleanse?
Will the shared air we breathe purge my lungs?
And will the waters still and find their calm
Or will a Tsunami be unleashed upon the land?

THE RISING SUN

The sun will rise without fail
Come thunder, come storm, come hail
On you it may rain, an endless rain
And so much pain,
And yet
The sun will rise again
Tomorrow

You may not see it shine
You may not feel the warmth of its rays
It may sit behind clouds
Grey like your mood
But it will rise without fail
On that you can count
Though the night may feel endless
And you may think you belong in the dark,
You don't.
Your eyes were not made to hunt
You were not born with such sight
You were made for the day
The one which won't stay away

On many things you cannot count
But the day, the sun and its return are certain
Its number in hours
Can be ticked off on fingers;

Awaiting in the dark
Luminous digits on a clock glare
There is no ticking and if
You closed your eyes, drifted off
Into slumber, it would come more quickly

But the night and its silence you consider your friend
The day, the sun and its return
Remind you that life goes on –
That people are happy going about their business.

You feel like visible scars are etched on your skin,
talon marks of your pain,
your loss,
but no one knows,
no one sees.
The world continues its trajectory.
It is not off kilter, unbalanced;
it is not teetering, about to fall.
People, like ants and bees, buzz about
busying themselves with the everyday,
with the ordinary, the inane
while you
you feel like you're slightly insane
quietly so
possibly the worst kind
because they wouldn't have seen it coming
when you slip off your chair
spit dribbling down the side of your mouth

unable even to wipe it off
when the life that was once visible in your eyes has gone
and you have slipped off to somewhere dark,
dark and lovely
an endless maze, stuck inside it,
inside your head,
forever,
never to return.
They'd speak of you,
Around you,
While you sat there staring off into that
Forever land
That corner of your mind
Thinking that you can't hear them

But you can
Their words like arrows will stab at your heart
All the tender bits of you exposed by life's hardships
Its beatings,
Its sandpaper rubbing
Raw your skin from its relentless scraping,
Raw your nails,
Raw your heart,
And their voices penetrate through, but you can't access them
They vibrate, echo off the cavernous
    space that is now your mind
If you could locate them singly
Maybe you could follow them home
Maybe you could find your way out

But they don't speak to you
They speak about you
Around you
And that leaves no path to follow

A MOMENT IN TIME

I stood still in the doorway
Still as the night
Afraid to cross the threshold
Afraid it might bite

I stood still in the doorway
What lay beyond?
I could not see in the darkness
nor could I respond

I stood still in the doorway
A certain unease
Listening yet quiet
Afraid even to breathe

I stood still in the doorway
How will this end?
I'm standing alone
But just maybe a friend
Could join me in the doorway
Push gently on my back
As I boldly step forward into the black

If you just believe
Anything is possible
What will you receive?

THE MOON AND I

It's dark and I can just see the sliver of the moon
    as it emerges from behind grey clouds.
It stares at me unblinking and I take a
    moment to stare back in return.
The moon and I, both contemplating the
    other, is how I imagine it.
Even as a little girl I loved the idea of the man in the moon and
    always pictured him as cheerful, with just a hint of sadness,
a kind of melancholy,
the kind that I now feel as I head out onto
    the path that will take me away.
Away from all that is familiar and comfortable,
away from constancy and certainty,
away from mundane and stress free.
To what, I don't yet know!
Will it be a life of passionate misery,
an ebb and flow of pain and joy?
Highs and lows like a little girl on a swing?
The moon stares on unwavering,
its slice a perfect banana shape,
only giving a glimpse of what it was,
yet I know that the moon holds so much more.
A full perfect round circle of a moon is there,
hidden now but it exists and so do I.
I exist as that full round moon does, yet so
    far all that's been visible is a sliver.

Well, not anymore!

WHO I AM

When at last you can look at yourself and say
Today **is** going to be a great day
Regardless of how you feel about who you think you are
Or who you think you are not
Regardless of the dimple on your chin and
    your possibly over-haughty grin
When you can know that it's not your outer exterior but
    your inner dialogue that's the heroine of your way
When you can with utter confidence say
I am who I am and that's okay

Light and happy heart
In forest glades I wander
Mysterious trees

Doorway

I have stood in the doorway between day and night,
The bright sunlight before me.
I have felt its warmth on my skin;
it beckons me in.
Behind me are the shadows of my former self,
the broken pieces I keep puzzling to fit together
as if by completing the puzzle I will understand.
But I'm missing the point.
In the shadows of the darkness there is only brokenness,
jagged edges and missing pieces.
In the dew of a morning sunlight even cobwebs sparkle.
I have known the day,
felt God's loving touch,
seen His works,
been comforted by His hand,
carried when I just couldn't
And yet still I hover in the doorway.
Today I choose to cross the threshold
into the fullness of all that He has for me,
into His unconditional love.
I will trust, fall into the light – and I will choose to stay.

I AM

I am shades of colour
I am reflections
I am broken glass
I am made new
I am shadows
I am light
I am history
I am bright
I am tomorrow
I am today
I am forgive me
I am please stay
I am the whispers in the darkness
I am the secrets in the night
I am let go
I am hold me tight

FAKE NEWS

Fake News,
Fake boobs,
Social media blues!
It's all so untrue,
It's not me, it's you!

It's not you, it's me,
There is no such thing as we!

Does he love me too?
One often asks a daisy
As the petals fall

TO WRITE

I sat down to write.
Not a thing had I to say
But silly bits and bobs and
Words that went astray
If only I could rhyme
I'd Insta all the time
The words that made such sense
Not those that were a mess
But alas it is not so
And to bed I shall have to go
My silly words and upturned
Thoughts no longer free to roam

THE ORDER

The date comes after
The wait comes first
The order is all wrong
I'm playing ping pong
With a song that reminds me of you on my mind
Back and forth, back and forth
This pointless rhythm
You drop a catch and it's quiet
Until one of us picks up the ball
And the game begins again

RE-ARRANGE

I have re-arranged my furniture,
the clothing in my cupboard,
the lamp in the corner,
the contents of my desk,
my handbag
but
I cannot re-arrange my life in a way that fits,
that fits me in.
Am I the odd piece that doesn't quite work,
when everything else has found its rightful place?
Will I keep spending my time re-arranging?
My office,
the boot of my car!
When will I be content with what is?

DISJOINTED

Carved together, torn apart, the fragments of my broken heart
Disjointed
Bone crushed, body bruised, aching from being used
Disjointed
Head turned, cast aside, straight arrow, no lies
Disjointed
How to heal? Know how I feel?
Disjointed
Screaming aloud, far too proud!
Disjointed
Shout it out, give a fuck, and leave me alone when I am stuck!

LAMPSHADE

She stands alone in the corner of the room,
once tall and proud,
now bent to one side,
her cords are worn
or she is torn
and the light that once shone is out.
The bulb is at an awkward angle to her erect form,
as if her neck has been broken.

She stands alone.

No-one has tried to switch her on;
it is as if they have forgotten her.
Yesterday they picked up the shade,
the one that once adorned her,
like a beautiful headdress
and she thought,
maybe they would put it on once more.
But it was moved away, out of sight,
So she felt even more naked than before,
naked and forgotten.

Alone she stands with so much light to offer the room,
if only she would be switched on.
Alone she stands,
Her potential unused,

her worth tarnished,
her head bowed and crooked.
She stands, feeling like a freak,
her self-esteem crushed.
Will someone take the time to see her?
Will someone take the time to see her for what she could be?

FEELINGS

Feelings lie,
they're deceptive
and they fool you into believing something
    that's not necessarily true.
The truth, on the other hand, is cold,
it's hard and it's weighty;
it's something that you can hold in the palm of your hand.
Something tangible,
not flighty like dandelions that disappear at
    the slightest whisper of wind.
No, truth holds firm.
The only question to be asked is,
what version of truth is real – yours or mine?

YOU CAN'T HAVE HAPPY

You can have all the finery in the world
A beautifully set table
A well-stocked kitchen
The "right" guests, who come for the finery
You can have laughter and merriment
You have wine on your table after all!
But you can't have happy, if it's not in your soul
You can't buy happy at the corner store
They don't sell that for real anymore
You can get it in a pill, but it's a temporary fill
and then you're ill at the thought of what you've done
how you've become undone – again
you bemoan your lack of self-discipline and you say
why does it have to be this way?
but it doesn't
and you don't
because you're looking for happy in the wrong places
and she's not there, trust me – it doesn't
    matter how long you stare
so open your heart, it's the right start
let God's love in and then you will see
what it truly is to be
happy

RAIN

She walks on silent streets
The darkness enfolds her
The rain falls gently, sweetly
A quiet rain, a deceptive rain
That mats her hair and trickles down her cheeks
Her hands in her pockets,
Her head down to prevent the rain from
Reaching her already wet eyes
She walks on, seemingly unaware,
Oblivious to the soaking of her
Clothes against her skin as the deceptive,
    constant rain falls relentlessly
She knows not when it will end!

QUESTIONS

I lie awake at night, staring at the barren ceiling.
It offers me nothing:
no condolences,
no solace,
and no remorse.
Its stark white façade is a harsh portrayal of the truth
that sometimes
there are no answers to the questions that keep us up at night.
Sometimes,
there is only the bleak emptiness.
Sometimes,
the ceiling we put above us stops us from going further,
limits us with our unanswered questions,
as if our expectations have all been placed there
and, when they return void,
we are left feeling helpless and alone.
But, if we were able to see beyond the ceiling
to the vast sky above,
to the myriad of stars in the universe,
we would have a glimpse of the triviality of
    our question in the first place
and we would be in awe and wonder
at the possibilities of what is and what could be.
It would be the beginning of our story and not the end.

BEAUTY, WHO IS SHE?

Beauty, who is she and why do we seek her out?
Is it the long tendrils of her hair, rather than a
    short stubby snout, we find so appealing?
Is it the way she looks?
Or the way she makes us feel?
Is there something in her smile, or is it
    the tress of her golden hair?
Beauty, who are you and will you linger on, when
    time has faded and fear has gone?
Beauty, art thou with me?
And how will I know?
I think you truly are a subjective thing,
    and so I will sing a new song.
One of acceptance and grace, and I will look into
    that space and fill it with love instead.

Refrigerator
Hums alone, a light goes on
Morning family

POETRY?

What is poetry? But words on a page!
What is a story? But a vision we've made.
What is art? But that which the eye will see!
What is beauty? But that which one holds in one's heart.
What is sorrow? But darkness personified.
What is grief? But sorrow in action.
What is pain? But hearts torn apart!
What is true love? But God!

STAR STRUCK

star struck
moonbeams in a faded light
memories of what has come and gone
so near so far
my dreams are real but
daylight lingers on
come steal the night away with me
my love so real so free
I hope you know this moment cannot last
for all eternity

THIS IS HOW

This is how
You belong
This is how
You solve the puzzle
This is how
You know you belong
This is how
Your mind works after all
This is your
Creativity
This is you
This is your breathing space
This is your happy place
This is no coincidence
This is not your undoing
But your beautiful mess
This is your opportunity
To creatively construct
To build wings
To fly
To soar
This is your open field
This is your dreamscape
This is you!

THE TRAVELLER

Dear Traveller,
Why do you hurry?
Why have you not the time to stop and see me?
To appreciate the magnificence of my existence
The solidness of my trunk
My roots that travel so far beneath your feet
So deep into the earth you could not fathom
I leave you letters
Constantly
You scrunch them under your boots and pass on
Oblivious
Today you have brought a small person
This smaller person with shorter legs has
    forced you to slow down
They have stopped beside me
Their tiny hands on my trunk
I pour my wisdom of seeing into them
But already they are wise, far wiser than you
Already they know things of observing
Of seeing all there is possible to see
They are curious and hungry for answers
For understanding
They know the importance of stopping
To watch the regiment of ants trudging
    along a fallen limb of mine,
Long since replaced

The wonder of watching the butterfly, the bee,
    sipping nectar or collecting pollen
From the flowers at your feet
The ones you barely notice
You
blinded by your busyness
The thoughts that occupy your mind
That keep you from the present
The here and now
from noticing the sky in a way other than
    to determine if it might rain.
You
who so deeply need to drink of the healing that is my world,
the great outdoors, nature – where God lives and breathes.
As you stand and wait for the child to finish its childish things,
how you see it.
I watch you.
You lift your head
and look up
as a bird on one of my branches begins to sing.
You close your eyes,
just briefly,
I see the glow of the sun warming your skin.
I see your face change
from disinterested to interested.
You open your eyes and look at me.
Really look at me
and even though it is not Autumn now
and I would like to keep myself fully clothed,

I let one of my leaves fall.
A letter just for you.
It falls slowly from just above your head
and I watch as you watch
its slow trajectory toward the earth,
its feather-like fall on this still afternoon.
It glides right past your face
but you do not reach out your hand and try to catch it,
like the child would have done.
No, you watch it fall
    to the ground,
and for a moment I am disappointed.
But then you bend down
and you pick it up,
your letter,
my leaf,
and I smile as I watch you turn it over in your hand
and begin to read my story.

HOW DO YOU?

How do you step off the mountain's edge,
knowing there is nothing below your feet?

How do you know your wings will grow at that very moment,
you take the committed step?

How do you know you won't fall,
But will fly?

How do you know, you will live,
not die?

You know because you must,
You know because you trust.

You know your maker,
Your caretaker.

You know because you know because He has promised
And because His promises are true.

Candyfloss so light
It's the colour of happy,
Explodes my senses

FREE PRISON

In my head I am free to dream
Free to roam,
nothing cast in stone
In my head I can run as fast as I want,
I can jump, I can fly, I can touch the sky
I am bigger and bolder and brighter
Then I could ever be
Yes, in my head I am free

This world is my prison
Here I'm confined,
there are rules –
you can't break them
there are walls – you can't shake them
my feet won't run nearly as fast
and all the good things don't really last.

This world is my prison
I am caged and I'm tethered
My days, they are measured
This world, it will use you
Bend you and bruise you
In this world I'm not safe,
I'm just a suffering waif

Fabulous forty
Where have the years disappeared
The future awaits

MOVING FORWARD

Sometimes it's not about how big the step is.
Sometimes it doesn't matter
that the ground won is minuscule
when compared
to the vast open plane before you

Sometimes it matters not that you
feel as though you're standing still
all the while trying to move forward

The emphasis is on the trying,
Whether that's a passionate drive
Managing to take steps while attached
At the waist to a bus or truck
Or
Whether you have only just
managed to put your shoes on

Both are wins
Both are victories to celebrate
Both are reminders of the longing

The dream
The willingness to get there
The other place that is not here.

There is filled with light and air and space
There has trees and leaves, a breeze that caresses your skin
And reminds you of the soul within

There is alive
There is a beehive
It's busy, it's industrious, it's creative
And the fruits of its labour is the sweetest honey

There is where you are meant to be
So DON'T stop moving forward.

WORDS LIKE RAIN

Words pour down like rain
On a parched landscape
They don't sit and pool and puddle
They disappear beneath the ground
Which remains as dry as before
Absorbed so completely are they
Until, at last, when enough
Positive, uplifting, encouraging
Words have been spoken
They hit the ground and bounce back up
Leaping and laughing
A joyful circus of loving
Healing, happy words.

TWO BIRDS

I wake to the birds each morning
Singing so sweetly of your goodness, Lord
Do they know of sorrow, when they sing always?
In Your creating of them You gave them a song
Do some refuse to sing and so deny the gift You've given?
Are some self-conscious of their voice then don't sing of the
    pure joy of a morning dawn or to greet their fellow birds?
No, each bird rises and sings out of their rising
They sing out to the glorious world that they
    are alive to sing for another day
They announce themselves saying "good
    morning", "good morning".
Whether it is or isn't they deem it so,
and so should we.
So should we rise as the birds do, early,
and greet the day
And say
I'm alive to live another
And go forth into it with that energy and that cheer
That resolution that all is and will be well.

THE CREEP

You try and you try to fall asleep
But in the thoughts creep
You toss, and you turn, and you moan
You reach for your phone,
IS THAT THE TIME?
So, you put on your light and say don't get a fright,
to your sleepy husband
You pick up your pen and open your friend,
a little notebook
so, you sit, and you write, though it's so late at night,
hoping to catch those thoughts that disturb,
that hatch and hatch, and multiply
too many you say oh do go away
but they replicate and complicate and
    even though it's late, it's late
the thoughts they can't wait.
I have tried very hard to capture them
With my pen and my book and my secret right hook
But with the light on they have scattered
Not one can I capture
So, what does it matter?
My sleep is disturbed, and you're not perturbed
I'll put away my weapon
I'll not look at the time
I'll switch off the light and maybe you're right
Sleep she will come,

She will not stay away
So, I yawn, and I stretch and off goes the light
Just maybe, good night.

WORDS

She wants to write like she's a poet, but she's not.
She wants to tattoo words on her forearm,
the curve of her waist,
her inner thigh,
collar bone,
neck,
all the places he could kiss and breathe fire into
    the words that already burn into her soul.
Branded there,
imprinted into the fabric of her being.
Words that turn her on,
that make her cry,
that make her sing.
Words with such power they root her to the ground,
so tangible she could touch them,
if she would just reach out her hand.

Yet words fail her constantly.
She cannot voice the words stored up inside,
huddled and hidden so well for that child who
    learned to play hide but don't seek.
Some games are not games,
neither are they fun.
No, she has no words but a million buried deep;
they're bubbling, a cauldron is gurgling after
    someone lit a fire in her belly.

It's not yet spilled over,
but it will and when it does no man will be able to silence her.
Words will pour forth like a steam train gaining
    momentum chugging out smoke,
like a slew of vomit after a drunken night.
Healing words!
Saving words!
Words the colour of summer or the grey of a rainy day.

GENDER ISSUES

Boy, girl you say?
What toy to play?
He or she
How do they pee?
What's wrong, what's right?'
Late into the night we ask ourselves these silly questions
What does it matter?
Who really cares!
If someone is different, why the stares?
A boy or girl is meant to be that,
But sometimes they want to wear a different hat.
Sometimes they're proud, sometimes they're loud,
Sometimes they don't want to stand out in the crowd.
But they don't have a choice, they're different you see
Different from you, different from me
Oh why in the world can't we just let them be?

MOONLIGHT BLISS

There beneath the moonlight bliss
Two dragons lay after a kiss
Her eyes were open
His were closed
Content to just lie and doze
She content to just lie and stare
Upon the beast for whom she'd come to care
He, feeling her eyes upon him look
Opened his and into him took
Her in a deep embrace
So, he too could look upon her face
Into each other's eyes they stared
And shared 10 000 stories there
Until, at last, the trance was broken with
Not a word between them spoken.

TIME

The sands of it visible in the hourglass turned don't trickle
They pour
The little pile of it not yet balanced
by the one above which still gives more.
Soon they will be even
and then the scales will tip
as time passed exceeds what's left
and when the glass is empty
and time itself is done

what then?

ABOUT THE AUTHOR

Melissa has a dream that she carries around on rumpled paper stuffed into her pocket. That dream is to write for a living, to spend her days stringing words together like Christmas decorations, bringing joy to young and old alike.

www.ingramcontent.com/pod-product-compliance
Lightning Source LLC
Chambersburg PA
CBHW031523040426
42445CB00009B/375